# Dedication

We would like to dedicate this book to our youngest
"Kid Concoctions" family member:

Christian John Thomas
born March 2001

"May you live a life full of the love, happiness and creativity we inspire to share."

# Acknowledgments

We would like to thank the children, parents, grandparents, educators, and all the others who have supported Kid Concoctions and helped it grow into more than we ever dreamed possible.

Other titles by John and Danita Thomas:

"The Ultimate Book of Kid Concoctions"  (ISBN# 0966108809)
"The Ultimate Book of Kid Concoctions 2"  (ISBN# 0966108817)
"The Ultimate Book of Holiday Kid Concoctions"  (ISBN# 0966108833)

# Foreword

We are excited to share with you our fourth book in the Kid Concoctions series; Kid Concoctions & Contraptions.

This new book will show you how to make exciting new projects quickly, easily and inexpensively using only household items. Children of all ages will learn to quickly create concoctions and contraptions ranging from hot air balloons and hovercrafts to plastic bubbles and tasty taffy. It is our hope these all-new projects will provide hours of entertainment and enjoyment for children while they learn about science, art, and mathematics.

Over the years we have been fortunate to receive many wonderful awards for our Kid Concoctions book series, yet we believe our best reward comes from seeing many children grow up and blossom into caring, creative adults.

Happy Concocting!!
John E. Thomas & Danita Thomas

# CONTENTS

*Adult supervision is recommended for all projects and recipes.*

# SUPER BUBBLE OOZE

*This amazing concoction can stretch, bounce, and blow up like a balloon.*

## WHAT YOU WILL NEED:

1/4 cup liquid laundry starch
1/4 cup school glue gel
1 drop food coloring

## HOW TO CONCOCT IT:

1. Pour school glue gel into a small bowl. Add 1 drop of food coloring and stir until blended.
2. Slowly pour the glue and food coloring mixture into a bowl containing 1/4 cup of liquid starch.
3. Let the mixture sit for five minutes. Remove it from the bowl and then slowly knead it with your hands until the glue absorbs almost all of the liquid starch. The more you knead your Super Bubble Ooze, the firmer it will become.
4. Store Super Bubble Ooze in a plastic zip bag or airtight container.

## CONCOCTION TIPS & IDEAS:

◆ Place a blob of Super Bubble Ooze on the end of a straw and blow it up like a balloon.
◆ Roll Super Bubble Ooze into a ball and see how high it will bounce.

# SODA POP POTION

*Our fizzing soda pop concoction will tickle your taste buds and astonish your friends.*

## WHAT YOU WILL NEED:

4 Tbs. lemon juice
2 tsp. baking soda
2 Tbs. confectioners' sugar
2 quarts cold water
4-6 drops food coloring

## HOW TO CONCOCT IT:

1. Stir water, food coloring, confectioners' sugar, and baking soda together in a pitcher until blended.
2. Stir in the lemon juice and your concoction should begin to fizz.

## CONCOCTION TIPS & IDEAS:

◆ Create multicolored ice cubes for your Soda Pop Potion by adding a few drops of food coloring to some water before freezing it in an ice cube tray.
◆ Make some color change magic by adding blue ice cubes to a yellow Soda Pop Potion. As the ice cubes melt, the soda will turn green!

# MOVIE GLASS CANDY

*Just like the breakable glass used in the movies, only you can eat it!*

## WHAT YOU WILL NEED:

2 cups sugar
1 cup water
Shallow disposable aluminum pan

## HOW TO CONCOCT IT:

1. Mix sugar and water together in a small saucepan.
2. With the help of an adult, stir the mixture over medium heat until the sugar is dissolved and the mixture is completely clear.
3. Remove the saucepan from the stove and let the liquid cool.
4. Pour the mixture into a shallow disposable aluminum pan.
5. Within 7-10 days the liquid will turn into a sheet of sugar glass.
6. Drain the remaining liquid from the pan. Carefully remove the sugar glass from the pan and place it on several layers of paper towels.
7. Break the Movie Glass with a small hammer and enjoy a tasty candy treat.

## CONCOCTION TIPS & IDEAS:

◆ Make Stained Glass Candy by stirring a few drops of food coloring into the candy mixture.
◆ Remember our Movie Glass is really candy. Real glass is dangerous and should never be eaten under any circumstances!

# PHONY SPILL

*This Phony Spill looks so real that even mom won't know it's really fake.*

## WHAT YOU WILL NEED:

1/2 cup white school glue
1 Tbs. poster paint or tempera paint
Paper cup
Wax paper

## HOW TO CONCOCT IT:

1. Mix glue and paint together in a small bowl.
2. Pour the mixture into a paper cup.
3. Lay the paper cup on its side on top of a large sheet of wax paper. This will form the Phony Spill.
4. Let the Phony Spill dry on the wax paper 1-2 days or until completely dried.
5. Slowly peel the dry Phony Spill and cup from the wax paper.
6. Phony Spill is most effective when placed on the floor or counter top. Never place Phony Spill on fabric or carpet.

## CONCOCTION TIPS & IDEAS

◆ Use a chocolate syrup can, mustard bottle, or ketchup bottle in place of the paper cup.
◆ Try placing a drinking straw or other objects in the Phony Spill to make it even more realistic.

# POCKET ROCKET

*You don't have to be a rocket scientist to create this pocket size rocket.*

## WHAT YOU WILL NEED:

1/2 Tbs. baking soda
2 Tbs. vinegar
35mm film container (with snap-on lid)
Small square of toilet tissue

## HOW TO CONCOCT IT:

1. Pour baking soda in the center of the tissue square. Roll the tissue around the soda and twist the ends.
2. Drop the soda filled tissue into the film container.
3. Have an adult pour the vinegar in the film container. QUICKLY snap the lid on the container and STAND BACK.

## CONCOCTION TIPS & IDEAS:

◆ Decorate your Pocket Rocket with markers or stickers.
◆ Have a contest to see whose Pocket Rocket can fly the highest.
◆ Experiment using different types of film containers; some tend to work better than others.
◆ Be sure to stand well away from your Pocket Rocket!

# JACK FROST CRYSTALS

*Duplicate the look of frost crystals on your windows regardless of the temperature outside.*

## WHAT YOU WILL NEED:

4 Tbs. Epsom Salt
1 cup stale beer
Facial tissue

## HOW TO CONCOCT IT:

1. Mix salt and beer together in a small bowl until the salt is partially dissolved.
2. Dip facial tissue into the mixture and wipe it evenly over a glass window.
3. While the window is still wet pat a moist tissue over the glass.
4. As the mixture dries, beautiful crystals will begin to grow.
5. Crystals will continue to grow for up to 24 hours.

## CONCOCTION TIPS & IDEAS:

◆ Add color to your crystals by adding 1 drop of food coloring to the salt and stale beer mixture.
◆ Jack Frost crystals can be washed off most windows with a cloth and some warm water.

# MAGIC EGG WRITING

*With this concoction any message you write on the outside of an eggshell will disappear and then reappear inside the egg.*

## WHAT YOU WILL NEED:

1 cup white vinegar
1 Tbs. alum (Found in the spice section of most grocery stores.)
Egg
Fine tip paintbrush

## HOW TO CONCOCT IT:

1. Mix white vinegar and alum together in a small bowl.
2. Dip the brush into the mixture and write a message on the eggshell.
3. Let the shell dry completely and then have an adult boil the egg for 15 minutes.
4. Let the boiled egg cool.
5. Peel off the egg shell and the message will appear inside the egg.  DO NOT EAT THE EGG!

## CONCOCTION TIPS & IDEAS:

◆ Put on a magic show for your friends. Pass the egg around and let everyone examine it. They will be amazed when you peel off the shell to reveal a message or even one of their names.

# SILLY SCENTS

*Use this concoction to create your own custom brand of perfume or cologne.*

## WHAT YOU WILL NEED:

2 Tbs. rubbing alcohol
1 Tbs. grated lemon peel
(you can also use one or more of
the following: grated orange peel,
cloves, rose petals, vanilla bean
or mint leaves)
1 plastic 35mm film container with
snap-on lid (wash before using)

## HOW TO CONCOCT IT:

1. Place grated lemon peel into the plastic film container.
2. Pour rubbing alcohol on top of the lemon peel.
3. Place the lid on top of the film container and shake.
4. Let the mixture set for several days, shaking it at least once a day.
5. The perfume/cologne is ready to wear when it smells like the scent you created and not like alcohol.

## CONCOCTION TIPS & IDEAS:

◆ Create a custom label for your Silly Scents using markers or stickers.
◆ Pour your Silly Scents mixture into a small fancy bottle, tie a ribbon around it and give as a gift.

# PICKLE POTION

*With this clever concoction you can transform cucumbers into pickles in just a few hours.*

## WHAT YOU WILL NEED:

1 large washed cucumber
1 Tbs. sugar
2 Tbs. salt
1 cup cider vinegar
Fork

## HOW TO CONCOCT IT:

1. Use the prongs of a fork to make deep, lengthwise grooves in the skin of the cucumber.
2. Have an adult slice the cucumber as thin as possible. Paper-thin slices work best.
3. Pour salt into a bowl. Toss the cucumber slices around in the bowl until they are completely covered with salt.
4. Place an airtight cover on top of the bowl. Let the mixture sit for one hour at room temperature.
5. Drain any liquid from the bowl.
6. Mix the sugar and vinegar together and pour it over the cucumbers.
7. Chill the cucumbers in the refrigerator for 3-4 hours and then serve.

## CONCOCTION TIPS & IDEAS:

◆ Try garnishing the pickles with dill before serving.
◆ Use the pickles on your favorite sandwich or by themselves as a snack.

# WACKY WATER CYCLONE

*Easily create your own underwater cyclone using a few simple household items.*

## WHAT YOU WILL NEED:

2 two-liter bottles
Plastic tape or duct tape
Water

## HOW TO CONCOCT IT:

1. Fill one two-liter bottle 3/4 of the way full with water.
2. Place the second bottle upside down on top of the first bottle.
3. Securely tape the two bottles together where they meet.
4. Turn the bottles upside down so the bottle full of water is on top.
5. Quickly move the bottles in a circular motion, and an underwater cyclone should appear.

## CONCOCTION TIPS & IDEAS:

◆ Add glitter or food coloring to the water before taping the two bottles together.
◆ Decorate the bottom of each bottle to look like a cityscape or farm scene.

# CRAZY RUBBER BONES

*Turn chicken bones into rubber using this simple kitchen concoction.*

## WHAT YOU WILL NEED:

Clean chicken bones
(drum sticks & wishbones work best)
White vinegar
Jar and lid

## HOW TO CONCOCT IT:

1. Place chicken bones in the jar.
2. Pour white vinegar over the chicken bones until they are completely covered.
3. Screw the lid onto the jar and let it sit for 7 days.
4. After 7 days remove the bones from the vinegar. The bones will look as though they have turned into rubber.

## CONCOCTION TIPS & IDEAS:

◆ Try using large turkey legs instead of chicken legs.
◆ Add a few drops of food coloring to the vinegar and the bones will change colors.

# MAGIC MOVIE BLOOD

*Make fake blood just like the kind used in many Hollywood movies.*

## WHAT YOU WILL NEED:

1 cup light corn syrup
10 drops red food coloring
1 drop blue food coloring
1 Tbs. water

## HOW TO CONCOCT IT:

1. Mix corn syrup and water together in a small bowl until well blended.
2. Add red and blue food coloring to the mixture and stir until blended.

## CONCOCTION TIPS & IDEAS:

◆ Make alien blood by using green food coloring instead of red and blue.

# INDOOR HOT AIR BALLOON

This amazing contraption will actually float in the air just like a real hot air balloon.

## WHAT YOU WILL NEED:

Tissue paper (the kind used in shirt boxes)
Glue stick
Scissors
Hair dryer

## HOW TO CONCOCT IT:

1. Cut the sheet of tissue paper so it looks like the example shown on the next page. (See diagram #1)
2. Use the glue stick to attach the angled tabs to the straight edge of the tissue. (See diagram #2)
3. Use the hair dryer to inflate the balloon with hot air. After a minute or so the balloon should float up into the air. Never let the hair dryer touch the tissue.
4. Should your balloon begin to topple over when it starts to float, add 3 paper clips around the bottom to help weight it down.

## CONCOCTION TIPS & IDEAS

◆ Use color markers to decorate your hot air balloon.
◆ Have a contest with your friends to see whose hot air balloon will float the highest.

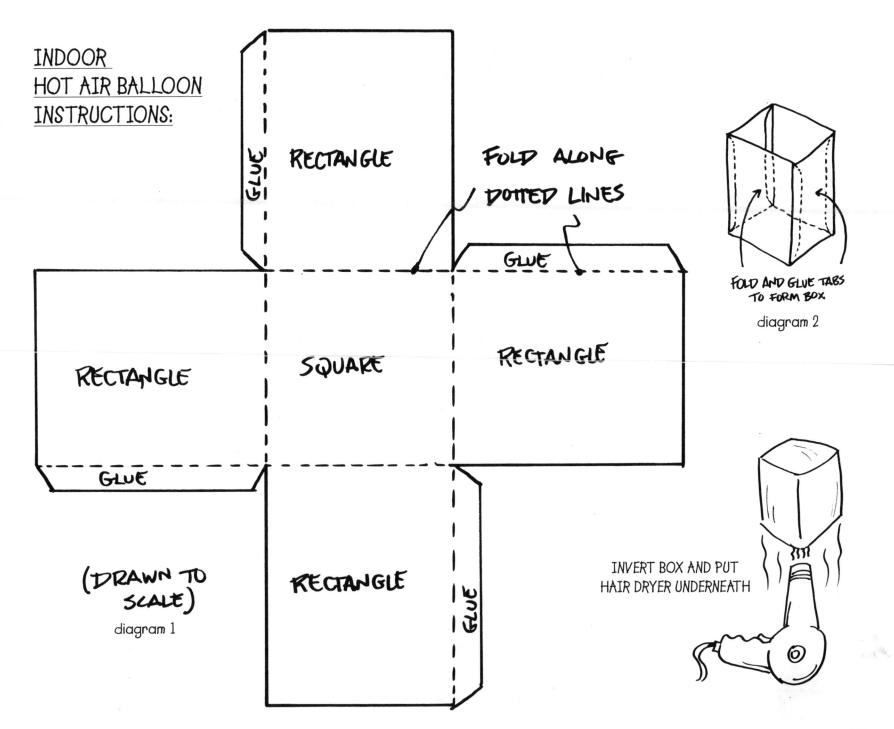

# INDOOR
# HOT AIR BALLOON
# INSTRUCTIONS:

GLUE

RECTANGLE

FOLD ALONG DOTTED LINES

GLUE

RECTANGLE

SQUARE

RECTANGLE

GLUE

RECTANGLE

GLUE

FOLD AND GLUE TABS TO FORM BOX

diagram 2

(DRAWN TO SCALE)

diagram 1

INVERT BOX AND PUT HAIR DRYER UNDERNEATH

# PLASTIC GELATIN

*With this concoction you can create homemade plastic that looks like stained glass.*

## WHAT YOU WILL NEED:

1 envelope unflavored gelatin
4 drops food coloring
3 Tbs. hot water
Disposable pie tin

## HOW TO CONCOCT IT:

1. Mix unflavored gelatin and hot water together in a small bowl until the gelatin is completely dissolved.
2. Add food coloring and stir until blended.
3. Pour the mixture into a disposable pie tin.
4. Let the mixture dry for 2-3 days or until the edges are hard.
5. Peel the Plastic Gelatin from the pie tin and cut it into a shape using scissors.

## CONCOCTION TIPS & IDEAS:

◆ Use Plastic Gelatin to create a mobile, sun catchers, guitar pick or book marker.
◆ Try adding a little bit of glitter to the Plastic Gelatin mixture before it dries.

# DIVING RAISINS SODA

*Turn a dull glass of soda pop into a mini tank of scuba diving raisins.*

## WHAT YOU WILL NEED:

1 glass clear soda pop (ginger ale, club soda etc.)
Raisins

## HOW TO CONCOCT IT:

1. Add several raisins to the glass of clear soda pop.
2. Watch as the raisins dive and resurface just like little scuba divers.

## CONCOCTION TIPS & IDEAS:

◆ Add 1 tsp. of baking soda to your glass of soda and the raisins will dive and resurface even faster.

# CRYSTAL PAINT

*With this cool concoction you can create sparkling pictures made of real crystals.*

## WHAT YOU WILL NEED:

1/4 cup very warm water
3 tsp. salt
Paintbrush
Black paper

## HOW TO CONCOCT IT:

1. Mix water and salt together in a small bowl until salt is almost dissolved.
2. Use a paintbrush to paint a picture using the salt mixture on a black sheet of paper.
3. As the painting begins to dry, white sparkling crystals will begin to appear.

## CONCOCTION TIPS & IDEAS:

◆ Add a few drops of food coloring to your Crystal Paint and create sparkling colorful pictures.
◆ Use Crystal Paint to decorate holiday cards and wrapping paper.

# LIQUID LAYER ART

*It's just like sand art only you use different types of colorful liquids instead of sand!*

## WHAT YOU WILL NEED:

2-3 drops red food coloring
2-3 drops blue food coloring
1/4 cup water
1/4 cup olive oil
1/4 cup rubbing alcohol
Tall clear glass

## HOW TO CONCOCT IT:

1. Mix red food coloring and water together in a small bowl. Pour the liquid into a tall glass.
2. Slowly pour olive oil into the glass on top of the water.
3. Mix blue food coloring and rubbing alcohol together in a small bowl. Slowly pour the liquid into the glass on top of the olive oil.

## CONCOCTION TIPS & IDEAS:

◆ Try creating your Liquid Art in fancy bowls or bottles to create a real conversation piece.
◆ Experiment using other types of liquids colored with food coloring like corn syrup.

# CRAZY COMPASS

*With this concoction you can quickly and easily make your very own working compass.*

## WHAT YOU WILL NEED:

Sewing needle
Magnet
Tape
Wide, flat piece of cork
Plate filled with water

## HOW TO CONCOCT IT:

1. Magnetize the needle by stroking it with a magnet repeatedly in the same direction for 30 seconds.
2. Tape the needle to the center of the cork.
3. Float the cork in the center of the water filled plate.
4. The needle will always point north and south.

## CONCOCTION TIPS & IDEAS:

◆ Because a needle is used, this project requires the assistance and supervision of an adult.
◆ Create a more portable compass by floating your Crazy Compass in a shallow plastic glass filled with water.

# CRAZY COMPASS INSTRUCTIONS:

NEEDLE ON CORK

WATER IN PAN

MAGNET

# WACKY TATTOOS

*Make your own washable tattoos just like the ones found in those delicious boxes of caramel corn and peanuts.*

## WHAT YOU WILL NEED:

Paper towels
Washable markers
Water

## HOW TO CONCOCT IT:

1. Cut or tear the paper towel into small squares.
2. Use the washable markers to draw pictures and designs on the small squares of paper towels to make your Wacky Tattoos.
3. Wet the back of your hand and place your tattoo face down on your hand.
4. Using the palm of your other hand, firmly push on the back of the tattoo to transfer it onto your skin.
5. Wacky Tattoos can easily be removed with soap and water.

## CONCOCTION TIPS & IDEAS:

◆ Celebrate your favorite holiday by making holiday themed Wacky Tattoos to give your friends and family members.
◆ Have a Wacky Tattoo party. Make and trade tattoos with your friends.

# GOOEY GUM DROPS

*These tasty treats are sure to please even the most discriminating sweet tooth.*

## WHAT YOU WILL NEED:

4 Tbs. unflavored gelatin mix
1 cup cold water
1 cup heated fruit juice
3-4 drops peppermint extract
Food coloring
2 cups sugar

## HOW TO CONCOCT IT:

1. Mix gelatin, water, extract and food coloring together in a small bowl. Let the mixture stand for 5 minutes.
2. Add the heated fruit juice to the gelatin mixture. Stir until the gelatin is dissolved.
3. Pour the mixture into a small shallow baking pan.
4. Place the pan into the refrigerator overnight.
5. Cut the Gooey Gum Drops into small squares and then roll in sugar.

## CONCOCTION TIPS & IDEAS:

◆ Experiment by using different flavors of extract to make your Gooey Gum Drops.
◆ Match the flavor of extract used with the color of food coloring (yellow for lemon, red for peppermint, etc.).
◆ Ask an adult to help you heat the fruit juice.

# BUBBLING BREW FINGER PAINTS

*This wacky brew of foaming, bubbling finger paints will amaze kids of all ages.*

## WHAT YOU WILL NEED:

Solution A
1 Tbs. white vinegar
1 Tbs. clear liquid dish soap
4 drops food coloring
Solution B
1 Tbs. baking soda
1 Tbs. water

## HOW TO CONCOCT IT:

1. Mix vinegar, dish soap and food coloring together in a small bowl. (Solution A)
2. In another bowl, mix baking soda and water together. (Solution B)
3. Pour Solution B into Solution A. Instantly the paint will begin to bubble and foam.
4. Stir the mixture until the color is even and then paint.

## CONCOCTION TIPS & IDEAS:

◆ Try painting on the shinny side of inexpensive freezer paper. It works just as well as store bought finger painting paper.
◆ Make magic color change finger paints by coloring Solution A with red food coloring and Solution B with yellow food coloring. When you mix the solutions together, the paint will be orange.

# MAGIC MARBLE DIP

*Use this crafty concoction to create beautiful marbleized paper, envelopes and other items.*

## WHAT YOU WILL NEED:

Oil based enamel paints (model car & airplane
paint works best)
Paper
Disposable aluminum cake or lasagna pan
Toothpick
Water
Rubber gloves

## HOW TO CONCOCT IT:

1. Fill a disposable aluminum pan with 3 inches of water.
2. Pour 1 tsp. of oil-based paint into the water. Repeat this step using 2-3 other colors of paint.
3. Swirl the colors of paint together with a toothpick.
4. Put on your rubber gloves and quickly dip a sheet of paper into the water and then slowly pull it back out. The paper should be marbleized.
5. Let the sheet of paper dry for 24 hours.

## CONCOCTION TIPS & IDEAS:

◆ Try dipping other items like pens, pencils, and small objects into the marbleizing solution.
◆ Make an entire marbleized stationery set that includes paper, envelopes and a pencil or pen.

# BALLOON HOVERCRAFT

*This balloon-powered hovercraft will provide hours of fun.*

## WHAT YOU WILL NEED:

Old CD (compact disc)
9-inch balloon
Snap cap (from a bottle of liquid dish soap)

## HOW TO CONCOCT IT:

1. Pull the top of the snap cap off and push the bottom through the hole in the center of the CD.
2. Snap the top of the snap cap back on the bottom, so the CD is sandwiched in-between.
3. Blow up the balloon and stretch it over the closed snap cap.
4. Pull open the snap cap and the air from the balloon will lift the hovercraft off the ground and make it float.

## CONCOCTION TIPS & IDEAS:

◆ Decorate your balloon with felt tip markers to give your hovercraft a personalized look.
◆ Have a hovercraft race with your friends by using drinking straws to blow on the hovercraft and make it shoot across the ground.

# BALLOON HOVERCRAFT INSTRUCTIONS:

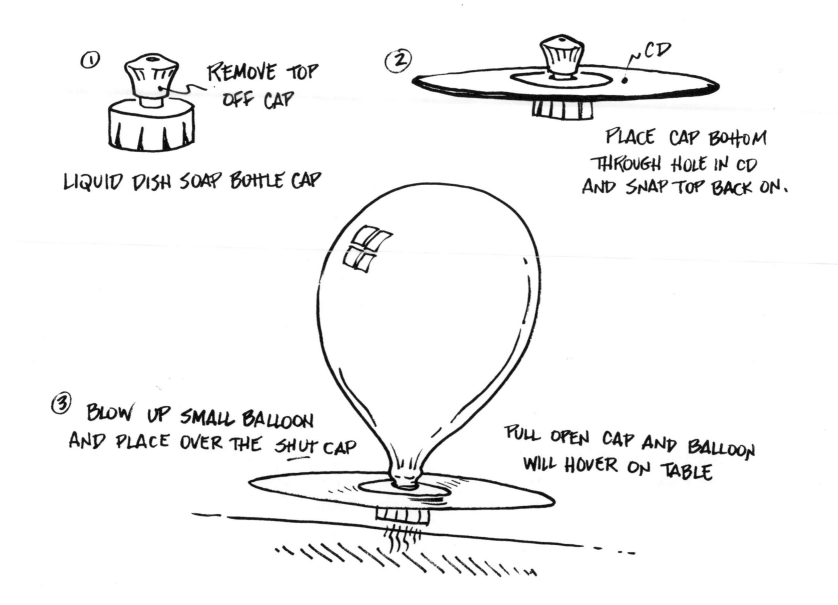

① REMOVE TOP OFF CAP

LIQUID DISH SOAP BOTTLE CAP

② ~CD

PLACE CAP BOTTOM THROUGH HOLE IN CD AND SNAP TOP BACK ON.

③ BLOW UP SMALL BALLOON AND PLACE OVER THE SHUT CAP

PULL OPEN CAP AND BALLOON WILL HOVER ON TABLE

# WACKY WINDOW PAINT

*This washable paint is perfect for creating awesome works of art on windows and large glass doors.*

## WHAT YOU WILL NEED:

2 Tbs. clear liquid dish soap
1 Tbs. poster paint or liquid tempera paint
Paintbrushes

## HOW TO CONCOCT IT:

1. Mix liquid dish soap and paint together in a small bowl.
2. Repeat the above step using several different colors of paint.
3. Dip your brush into the Wacky Window Paint and paint on a glass window or glass door. Be careful not to get paint on woodwork, caulking or any other non-glass surface.

## CONCOCTION TIPS & IDEAS:

◆ Remove Wacky Window Paint by wiping with a moist paper towel or old cloth.
◆ Use Wacky Window Paint to create window decorations for holidays throughout the year.

# GOOFY GEL AIR FRESHENER

*With this concoction you can make your own great smelling gel air freshener just like the ones sold in stores.*

## WHAT YOU WILL NEED:

2 envelopes unflavored gelatin (2 Tbs.)
15 - 20 drops perfume, cologne or other fragrance
1/2 cup hot water
1/2 cup ice-cold water
Food coloring
Baby food jar

## HOW TO CONCOCT IT:

1. Mix gelatin and hot water in a bowl until the gelatin is completely dissolved.
2. Stir in food coloring and fragrance.
3. Add ice-cold water and stir.
4. Pour the mixture in a baby food jar and let it set overnight at room temperature or until it turns into a gel.

## CONCOCTION TIPS & IDEAS:

◆ Do not place Goofy Gel Air Freshener in the refrigerator or the smell will be absorbed by your food.
◆ Decorate the baby food jars with ribbon, stickers or wrapping paper and give as a gift.

# PISTOL POPPER

*Children have created this classic Pistol Popper contraption for over 100 years.*

## WHAT YOU WILL NEED:

1 12 x 16 inch sheet of paper (cut from a brown paper bag)

## HOW TO CONCOCT IT:

1. Fold paper in half lengthwise. Then open it back up again.
2. Fold all four corners of the paper down to meet the center fold.
3. Fold paper in half along the center fold.
4. Fold paper in half and then open it back up.
5. Fold the largest corners of the paper down. (See illustration on page 39)
6. Fold the paper back to make a triangle shape.
7. Make your pistol pop by holding it by the points and then snapping it down through the air.

## CONCOCTION TIPS & IDEAS:

◆ Decorate your Pistol Popper using colored pencils, felt tip markers or paints.
◆ Pistol Poppers can be a fun and inexpensive activity for birthday parties.

# PISTOL POPPER INSTRUCTIONS:

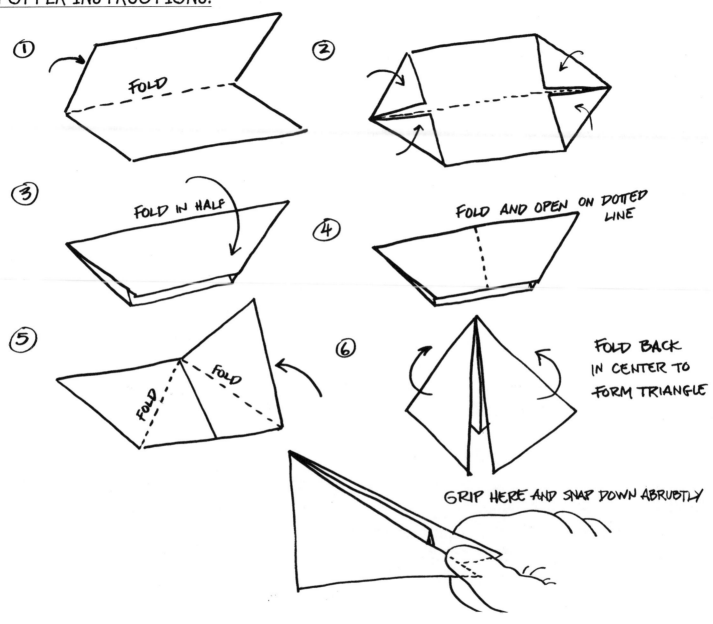

① FOLD

②

③ FOLD IN HALF

④ FOLD AND OPEN ON DOTTED LINE

⑤ FOLD FOLD

⑥ FOLD BACK IN CENTER TO FORM TRIANGLE

GRIP HERE AND SNAP DOWN ABRUPTLY

# HANDPRINTS IN THE SAND

*Capture your handprint and the feeling of being at the beach with this fun, easy to create concoction.*

## WHAT YOU WILL NEED:

Plaster of Paris
Water
Sand
Box

## HOW TO CONCOCT IT:

1. Fill your box with moist, hard packed sand.
2. Push both hands down into the sand to create an impression at least 1/2 inch to 2 inches deep.
3. Mix Plaster of Paris according to the directions on the package and then pour the mixture into the handprints.
4. Let the mixture set for 45 minutes and then remove the handprints from the sand.
5. Let the handprints dry in a sunny window for 1 hour.

## CONCOCTION TIPS & IDEAS:

◆ Make a hanger for your handprints by pushing a paper clip into the Plaster of Paris before it is completely dry.
◆ Use your feet to make footprints in the sand instead of handprints.

# RAIN PAINT

*Turn a rainy day into a fun day by actually painting with rain drops.*

## WHAT YOU WILL NEED:

Paper plate (uncoated)
Food coloring

## HOW TO CONCOCT IT:

1. Place several drops of food coloring on the plate.
2. Have an adult place the plate outside in the rain for 10 – 60 seconds. Time will vary depending on how fast the rain is falling.
3. Bring the plate indoors to dry.

## CONCOCTION TIPS & IDEAS:

◆ Try drawing a picture on the plate with a white crayon before adding food coloring.
◆ Experiment by substituting washable poster paint or tempera paint for food coloring.

# CRYSTAL FARM

*Grow real crystals in this amazing underwater garden.*

## WHAT YOU WILL NEED:

Small clear glass bowl
Assorted rocks, pebbles and seashells
2 ounces alum (found in the spice section of
most grocery stores)
1/2 cup hot water

## HOW TO CONCOCT IT:

1. Fill the clear glass bowl half full with rocks,
   pebbles or seashells.
2. Mix water and alum together until alum is
   completely dissolved.
3. Pour the mixture over the contents of
   the bowl.
4. Within a few hours crystals should begin to grow.
   After several days you should have many large crystals growing in your Crystal Farm.

## CONCOCTION TIPS & IDEAS:

◆ Try adding a few drops of food coloring to the water and alum mix to grow colored crystals.

# MARBLEIZED EGG DIP

*Create beautiful marbleized eggs with this quick and easy egg dip.*

## WHAT YOU WILL NEED:

Hard-boiled eggs
1 Tbs. vegetable oil
1 Tbs. food coloring
1 Tbs. white vinegar
2 cups water

## HOW TO CONCOCT IT:

1. Mix water, vinegar, and food coloring together in a small bowl.
2. Pour oil around on top of the mixture.
3. Dip the egg into the oil, water and food coloring mixture.
4. Let the egg sit in the mixture for several minutes and then slowly remove it from the liquid.
5. Let the egg sit until dry.

## CONCOCTION TIPS & IDEAS:

◆ When the egg dries, try repeating the above steps using the same egg and a different color of food coloring.
◆ Try using eggshells with the yolk blown out in place of hard-boiled eggs.

# DISAPPEARING EGG SHELL

*Turn ordinary hard-boiled eggs into rubber eggs using this simple science concoction.*

## WHAT YOU WILL NEED:

1 hard-boiled egg
1 jar with lid
White vinegar

## HOW TO CONCOCT IT:

1. Place the hard-boiled egg into the jar.
2. Fill the jar with white vinegar.
3. Screw on the lid and let the egg sit for 3 days.
4. After 3 days the eggshell will be gone leaving a thin white membrane. The egg will look and feel like rubber.

## CONCOCTION TIPS & IDEAS:

◆ This concoction is a great science experiment demonstrating the chemical reaction calcium carbonate (the egg shell) and vinegar have when mixed together.

# SANDPAPER TRANSFER ART

With Sandpaper Transfer Art you can make copies of your favorite crayon drawings to share with your family and friends.

## WHAT YOU WILL NEED:

Sandpaper
Crayons
White paper

## HOW TO CONCOCT IT:

1. Push down hard on your crayons and draw a picture on a piece of sandpaper.
2. Place the sandpaper, drawing side down, onto a sheet of plain white paper.
3. Have an adult iron the back of the sandpaper with an iron set on low.
4. Carefully peel the sandpaper off of the white paper to reveal a copy of your drawing.

## CONCOCTION TIPS & IDEAS:

◆ Use Sandpaper Transfer Art to create unique holiday cards and stationery.
◆ Try creating a picture with a white crayon and then transfer it to a black sheet of paper.

# UNCLE JOHN'S ANT FARM

*You won't believe how easy it is to make this amazing ant farm with just a few household items.*

## WHAT YOU WILL NEED:

Clear plastic 2-liter bottle with cap
Sand (enough to fill the bottle 3/4 full)
Water
Small pin
Ants from the same colony

## HOW TO CONCOCT IT:

1. Fill the bottle 3/4 full with sand.
2. Pour a little water in the bottle to slightly moisten the sand.
3. Have an adult use the pin to poke a series of air holes in the bottle.
4. Place the ants in the bottle and screw the cap on tight.
5. Watch as the ants begin to make tunnels.
6. Keep the sand moist with water and feed your ants daily using breadcrumbs or dead insects.

## CONCOCTION TIPS & IDEAS:

◆ Keep your ant farm out of direct sunlight.
◆ Give your ants an occasional special treat by feeding them a few drops of water and sugar mixed together.

# MINIATURE GREENHOUSE

Grow plants faster and healthier with this easy to make Miniature Greenhouse.

## WHAT YOU WILL NEED:

Clear 2-liter plastic bottle
Seeds
Peat moss
Flower pot
Pebbles or small rocks

## HOW TO CONCOCT IT:

1. Have an adult cut the plastic bottle in half. Use the top half for your greenhouse and save the bottom to create the Wacky Worm Farm found on page 50.
2. Place a handful of pebbles in the bottom of the flower pot.
3. Fill the flower pot with peat moss and then plant your seeds.
4. Water the soil and the seeds.
5. Place the top half of the bottle over the flower pot and put the greenhouse in a sunny spot.
6. Water your plant a few times a week or when the peat moss gets dry.

## CONCOCTION TIPS & IDEAS:

◆ Use brightly colored paints to decorate the flower pot and give your Miniature Greenhouse as a gift.
◆ Plant herbs in several Miniature Greenhouses to create your own indoor herb garden.

# INSTANT INTERCOM

*Talk to your friends or family members with this homemade intercom that works just like a telephone.*

## WHAT YOU WILL NEED:

Garden hose
Two medium size funnels
Black electrical tape

## HOW TO CONCOCT IT:

1. Make sure there isn't any water in the garden hose.
2. Push a funnel in each end of the hose.
3. Secure the funnels to the hose using black electrical tape.
4. Test your intercom by talking into one end while holding the other end to your ear.

## CONCOCTION TIPS & IDEAS:

◆ Use color plastic tape to decorate your instant intercom.
◆ Talk to your friends by stretching the intercom around corners, across the yard or even to a neighbor's house.

# INSTANT INTERCOM INSTRUCTIONS:

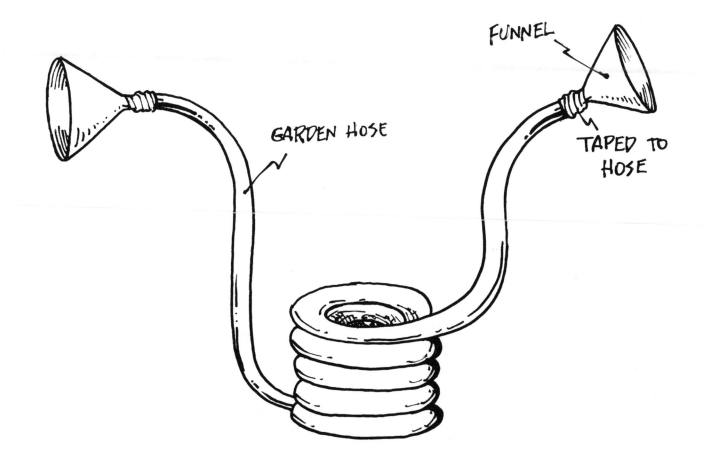

FUNNEL

TAPED TO HOSE

GARDEN HOSE

# WACKY WORM FARM

*With the Wacky Worm Farm you'll have fun observing earthworms as they dig, play and eat.*

## WHAT YOU WILL NEED:

Clear 2-liter plastic bottle
Soil
Sand
Pebbles or small rocks
Fresh leaves
Water
Earthworms

## HOW TO CONCOCT IT:

1. Have an adult cut the plastic bottle in half. Use the bottom half for your Wacky Worm Farm and save the top to create the Miniature Greenhouse found on page 47.
2. Layer the bottom of the bottle with pebbles.
3. Add sand and soil in alternate layers until the bottle is almost full.
4. Moisten the soil and sand with a little water.
5. Lay the earthworms on top of the soil and cover them with fresh leaves.
6. Put the Wacky Worm Farm in a dark place and keep the soil moist.

## CONCOCTION TIPS & IDEAS:

◆ Plant a few grass seeds or a mini plant in the worm farm. Observe as the worms pull the grass or plant leaves under the soil and eat them.

# BALANCING BUTTERFLY TRICK

This Balancing Butterfly Trick will amaze your friends and family members as you balance the butterfly on your fingertip or nose.

## WHAT YOU WILL NEED:

Paper
Cardboard
2 small coins
Tape
Scissors
Felt tip markers

## HOW TO CONCOCT IT:

1. Fold a sheet of paper in half and draw half of a butterfly, making sure that the bottom wing is larger and hangs lower than the top wing. It is important to do this step correctly so the butterfly will balance properly.
2. With the paper still folded, cut out the butterfly. Trace the paper butterfly on a piece of cardboard and then cut out the cardboard butterfly.
3. Decorate the butterfly wings with felt tip markers.
4. Turn the butterfly over and tape the coins to the widest part of each of the bigger wings.
5. Balance the butterfly on your finger, your nose, the corner of a table or on the eraser of a pencil. If your butterfly does not balance, try repositioning the coins.

## CONCOCTION TIPS & IDEAS:

◆ Create a real glitzy butterfly by decorating the wings with white school glue, glitter, and paint.
◆ Make several butterflies and give them as party favors.

# NATURAL PLANT PAINTS

*Create your own natural paints, just like the ones used in ancient times, using various different types of plants.*

## WHAT YOU WILL NEED:

Grass for green
Carrots for orange
Cranberries for pink
Dandelions or daffodils for yellow
Beets for red
Water

## HOW TO CONCOCT IT:

1. Have an adult boil each of the plants in a separate pot of water until the water turns to the desired shade or color.
2. Remove the water from heat and allow it to cool.
3. Separate into small paper cups or muffin tins and paint.

## CONCOCTION TIPS & IDEAS:

◆ Experiment making paints from spices (mustard, curry, red currants, paprika and cocoa) mixed with a little bit of water.

# GELATIN ORANGES

*These tasty treats look just like real orange wedges and make the perfect low fat snack.*

## WHAT YOU WILL NEED:

Oranges
1 box orange flavored gelatin

## HOW TO CONCOCT IT:

1. Have an adult cut the oranges in half and scoop out the center leaving the outer skin.
2. Prepare the box of orange gelatin by following the printed instructions on the package.
3. Instead of pouring the liquid gelatin into a bowl to gel, pour it into the orange halves.
4. Place the orange halves full of gelatin into the refrigerator to gel for 8 hours.
5. Remove the orange halves from the refrigerator and have an adult cut the oranges into wedges.

## CONCOCTION TIPS & IDEAS:

◆ Use different types of citrus fruit (grapefruit, lemons and limes) along with different flavors of gelatin to create unique tasty treats.
◆ Follow the directions on the package of gelatin, except try substituting orange juice in place of the water, to create gelatin oranges bursting with flavor.

# BLOOMIN' FLOWERS

*When you place these beautiful paper flowers in a bowl of water they begin to bloom and open up just like real flowers.*

## WHAT YOU WILL NEED:

Construction paper
Scissors
Crayons or felt tip markers
Small bowl of water

## HOW TO CONCOCT IT:

1. Draw a picture of a flower (using the illustration as a pattern) on a sheet of construction paper.
2. Color and decorate the flower using crayons or felt tip markers.
3. Cut out the flower and fold shut to form a bud.
4. Place the flower bud in a bowl of water.
5. As the paper absorbs the water, the flower bud will open.

## CONCOCTION TIPS & IDEAS:

◆ Create your own original patterns to make Bloomin' Flowers in a wide variety of shapes and sizes.
◆ Write messages in the center of your flower. As the flower blooms your message will be revealed.

# BLOOMIN' FLOWERS INSTRUCTIONS:

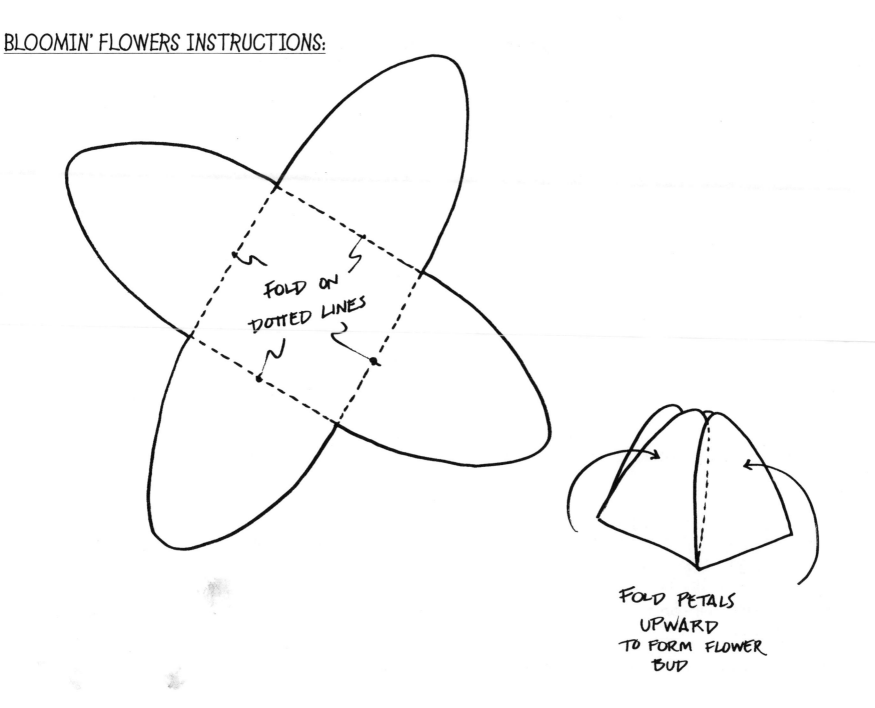

FOLD ON DOTTED LINES

FOLD PETALS UPWARD TO FORM FLOWER BUD

# SQUEEZE ROCKET

*Similar to the flying air rockets sold in stores only this one costs just pennies to make.*

## WHAT YOU WILL NEED:

Soft plastic squeeze bottle (dishwashing liquid, ketchup or mustard bottle works fine)
2 plastic straws, one narrower than the other
Tape
White school glue
Paper

## HOW TO CONCOCT IT:

1. Create your launch pad by making a hole in the cap of the squeeze bottle and pushing the small straw through it.
2. Squeeze white glue around the base of the straw to hold it in place and seal any cracks. Let the glue dry completely and then wrap with tape.
3. Make your rocket by cutting 4 inches off the larger straw.
4. Make fins for your rocket by cutting two small triangles out of paper and then attaching them to the straw with tape.
5. Seal the top of the rocket with tape. Continue wrapping the tape around the top of the rocket to form a nose cone.
6. Slide the large straw (rocket) over the small straw (launch pad) and then squeeze the bottle hard and fast to launch the rocket in the air.

## CONCOCTION TIPS & IDEAS:

◆ Decorate your rocket and launch pad using paints, felt tip markers or colored tape.
◆ Challenge your friends to a rocket race to see whose rocket goes the highest or the furthest.

# SQUEEZE ROCKET INSTRUCTIONS:

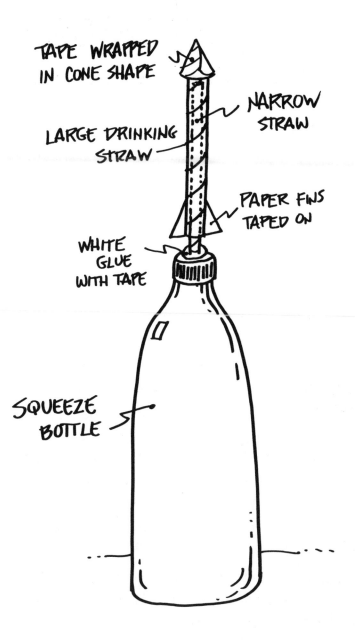

TAPE WRAPPED
IN CONE SHAPE

NARROW
STRAW

LARGE DRINKING
STRAW

PAPER FINS
TAPED ON

WHITE
GLUE
WITH TAPE

SQUEEZE
BOTTLE

# GYROCOPTER

*Just like a helicopter, this Gyrocopter spins and then launches into the air.*

## WHAT YOU WILL NEED:

Index card cut into a 4 inch square
Scissors
Tape
Thread spool
Thin stick
String

## HOW TO CONCOCT IT:

1. Trace the pattern to your right onto an index card.
2. Cut on the solid lines with scissors and fold on the dotted lines as shown in the illustration. One side of each rotor should be folded up and the other down.
3. Punch a small hole in the center of the square and push a narrow stick through it. Attach the stick firmly with tape.
4. Push the stick in the center of the thread spool and then wrap the string around the stick.
5. Quickly pull the string to make the Gyrocopter spin and take off into the air. You may have to try this step several times before your Gyrocopter flies.

## CONCOCTION TIPS & IDEAS:

◆ Decorate your Gyrocopter with crayons or colored pencils.
◆ Make a bulls-eye with a piece of paper and then have a contest with your friends to see whose Gyrocopter comes closest to the center of the bulls-eye.

# GYROCOPTER INSTRUCTIONS:

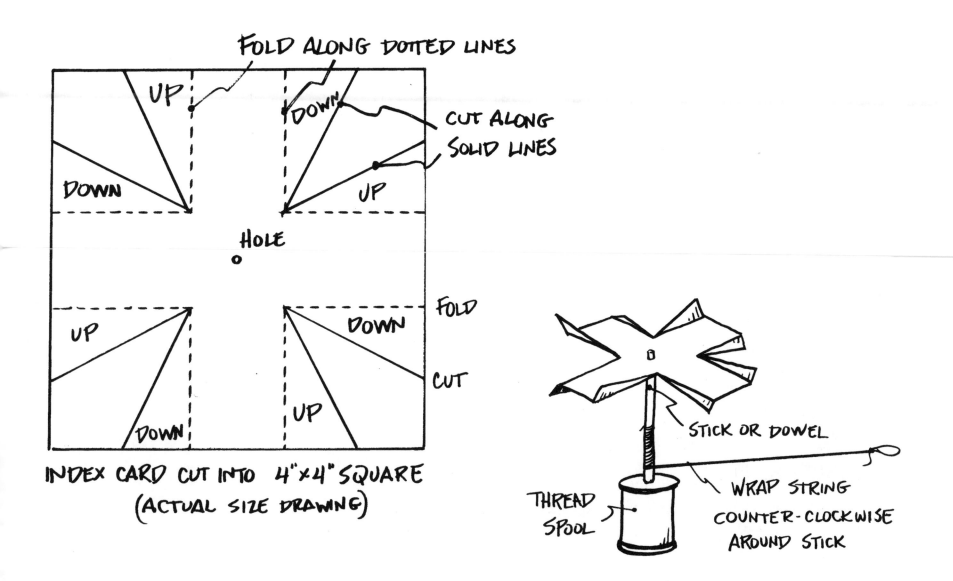

FOLD ALONG DOTTED LINES

UP

DOWN

CUT ALONG SOLID LINES

DOWN

UP

HOLE

UP

DOWN

FOLD

CUT

DOWN

UP

INDEX CARD CUT INTO 4"x4" SQUARE
(ACTUAL SIZE DRAWING)

STICK OR DOWEL

THREAD SPOOL

WRAP STRING COUNTER-CLOCKWISE AROUND STICK

# BALLOON RETROROCKET

*This quick and easy contraption will keep you entertained for hours.*

## WHAT YOU WILL NEED:

1 straw
1 oblong balloon
15 - 20 feet of string
Tape

## HOW TO CONCOCT IT:

1. Tie one end of the string to a chair, post or tree. Thread a straw through the other end of string and pull the string as tight as possible. Tie the string to another chair, post or tree.
2. Blow up the balloon and secure it to the straw using two pieces of tape.
3. Release the balloon and watch as it shoots down the line of string.

## CONCOCTION TIPS & IDEAS:

◆ Create 2 Balloon Retrorockets and have them race each other to see which one goes the furthest and the fastest.
◆ Decorate your Balloon Retrorocket with felt tip markers.

# BALLOON RETROROCKET INSTRUCTIONS:

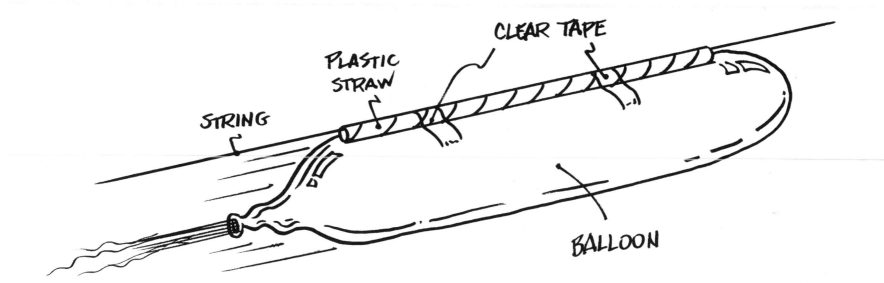

CLEAR TAPE

PLASTIC STRAW

STRING

BALLOON

# SANDY GLUE PAINT

*Create beautiful 3-D pictures with this unique and unusual concoction.*

## WHAT YOU WILL NEED:

Squeeze bottle or cake bag
1/2 cup glue
1/4 cup sand
2 Tbs. tempera paint or poster paint
Paper

## HOW TO CONCOCT IT:

1. Mix glue and sand together in a small bowl.
2. Stir in paint and continue mixing until the color is evenly blended.
3. Spoon the mixture into a squeeze bottle or cake bag.
4. Squeeze the mixture onto a sheet of paper to create a unique 3-D Sandy Glue work of art.

## CONCOCTION TIPS & IDEAS:

◆ Try making several different batches of Sandy Glue Paint using different colors of paint.
◆ If you don't have a squeeze bottle or cake bag, spoon the Sandy Glue into a zip bag and snip off a small piece of the corner with scissors. Squeeze the zip bag to paint.

# TASTY TAFFY

*This concoction captures the taste of old-fashioned taffy.*

## WHAT YOU WILL NEED:

1 cup sugar
1/4 cup water
2 Tbs. vinegar
1 Tbs. butter
1/2 tsp. vanilla

## HOW TO CONCOCT IT:

1. Mix the sugar, water, and vinegar together in a large pot.
2. Have an adult boil the mixture until it reaches the "hard ball stage" (a drop of the mixture turns into a ball when dropped in cold water.)
3. Stir in butter and vanilla and then pour the mixture into a shallow pan coated with butter.
4. Let the mixture cool for one hour.
5. Butter your hands and then twist, pull and fold the mixture until it becomes a creamy color and difficult to pull.
6. Roll the taffy into a long rope and then cut into small pieces and wrap in wax paper.

## CONCOCTION TIPS & IDEAS:

◆ Try adding a few drops of food coloring to the sugar, water, and vinegar mixture to make your taffy different colors.
◆ Put a handful of homemade Tasty Taffy into a glass jar and give as a gift.

# LOOPY FLYER

*Children of all ages will love this simple glider made of two strips of paper and a drinking straw.*

## WHAT YOU WILL NEED:

Tape
Drinking straw
1 inch x 7 inch strip of paper
3/4 inch x 6 inch strip of paper

## HOW TO CONCOCT IT:

1. Tape the ends of each strip of paper together to form two loops, one larger than the other.
2. Tape the small loop to one end of the straw and the large loop to the other end of the straw.
3. Hold the center of the straw, with the small loop facing forward and toss your Loopy Flyer into the air.

## CONCOCTION TIPS & IDEAS:

◆ Jazz up your Loopy Flyer by using colored paper to make the loops and a bright colored straw for the body of the glider.

# LOOPY FLYER INSTRUCTIONS:

PAPER LOOPS

PLASTIC STRAW

TAPED
TO STRAW

# HYDRO JET BOAT

*This Hydro Jet Boat is actually powered by carbon dioxide gas made by mixing vinegar and baking soda together.*

## WHAT YOU WILL NEED:

1 plastic 16 oz. soda bottle with cap
1/4 cup vinegar
1 Tbs. baking soda
Plastic straw
White glue

## HOW TO CONCOCT IT:

1. Ask an adult to poke a hole in the bottom edge of the plastic bottle.
2. Insert the straw into the hole, leaving 1 inch hanging out.
3. Seal the air cracks around the straw with white glue. Let the glue completely dry before continuing. Apply a second layer of glue if necessary.
4. Pour the vinegar into the bottle. Add baking soda and quickly put the cap back on the bottle.
5. Place the Hydro Jet Boat in a tub of water and watch it go!

## CONCOCTION TIPS & IDEAS:

◆ Add a few drops of red, blue, or green food coloring to the white vinegar. Observe what happens as the boat sails across the water.
◆ Make boats out of different colors of plastic bottles to create an entire fleet.

# HYDRO JET BOAT INSTRUCTIONS:

BAKING SODA

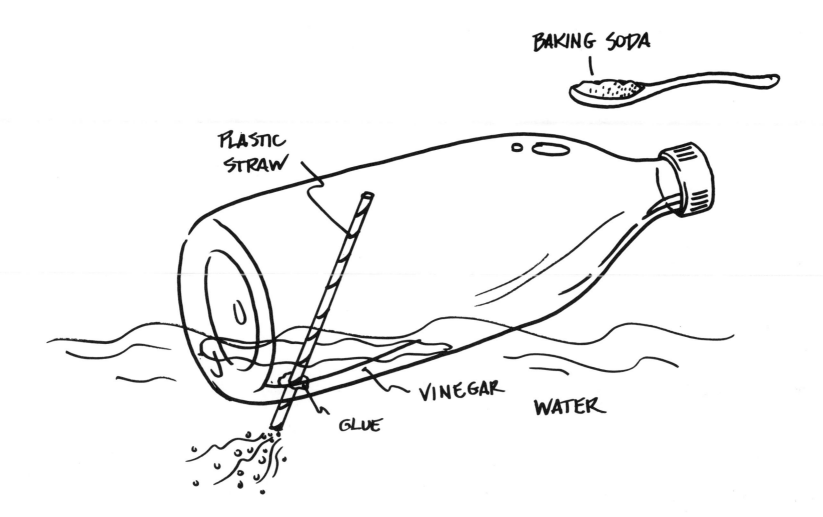

PLASTIC STRAW

VINEGAR

WATER

GLUE

# BALL BLASTER

*Launch ping-pong balls across the room and into the sky using this creative ball launcher.*

## WHAT YOU WILL NEED:

2 toilet paper tubes
Tape
Plastic wrap
1 rubber band
2 paper clips

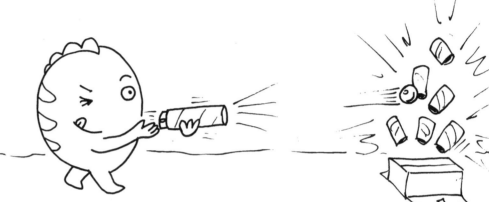

## HOW TO CONCOCT IT:

1. Cut one toilet paper tube lengthwise.
2. Put the toilet paper tube back together with tape, making sure it is now narrow enough to fit inside the other tube.
3. Tape plastic wrap on one end of the narrow tube.
4. Place the narrow tube inside of the uncut tube.
5. Place a paper clip on the end of each tube directly across from each other.
6. Attach one end of the rubber band to each of the paper clips (see the illustration).
7. Place the ping-pong ball inside the tube and pull the inner tube back and release it to launch the ball.

## CONCOCTION TIPS & IDEAS:

◆ Set up rows of decorated toilet paper tubes and then try to knock them over with your Ball Blaster.
◆ Decorate the ping-pong balls and your Ball Blaster using felt tip markers.

# BALL BLASTER INSTRUCTIONS:

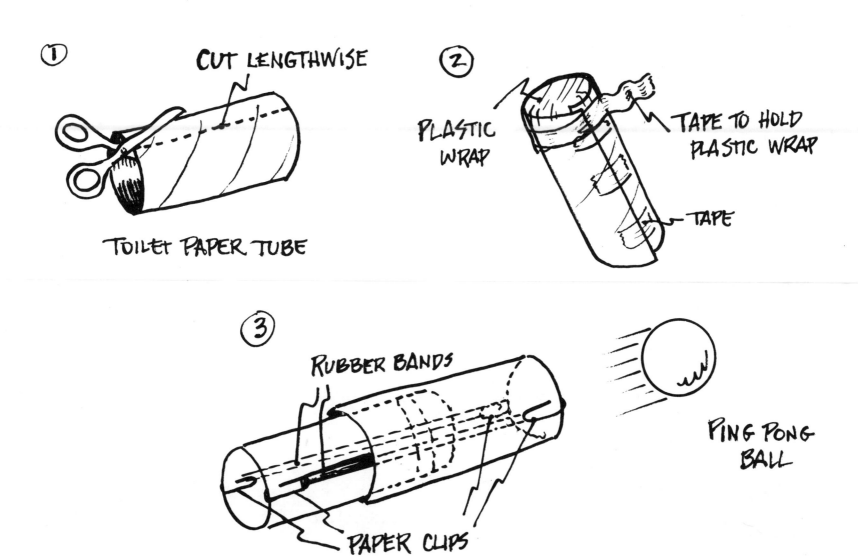

① CUT LENGTHWISE

TOILET PAPER TUBE

② PLASTIC WRAP

TAPE TO HOLD PLASTIC WRAP

TAPE

③ RUBBER BANDS

PAPER CLIPS

PING PONG BALL

# ROCKET SLIDER GAME

*This cool Rocket Slider Game should be played with a friend who's not afraid of some fun, fast paced rocket action.*

## WHAT YOU WILL NEED:

2 1-liter plastic soda bottles
Electrical tape
2 12-foot strings
2 plastic ring six pack can holders

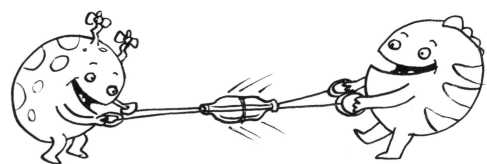

## HOW TO CONCOCT IT:

1. Have an adult cut both plastic bottles in half.
2. Tape the tops of both bottles together.
3. Thread both pieces of 12-foot string through the bottles.
4. Cut both plastic ring holders in half to make 4 two loop handles.
5. Tie a handle to each end of the string. You're ready to play!
6. Each player holds onto two handles and moves away from the other player until the strings are tight.
7. Pull the strings apart to launch the rocket toward the other player. Put your hands together to allow the other player to launch the rocket toward you.

## CONCOCTION TIPS & IDEAS:

◆ Decorate the outside of your rocket using construction paper, glue and felt tip markers.

# ROCKET SLIDER GAME INSTRUCTIONS:

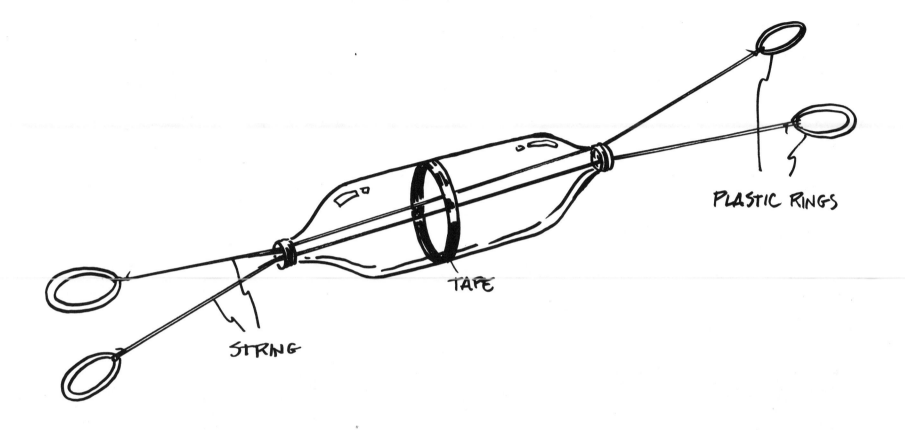

PLASTIC RINGS

TAPE

STRING

# WHIRLY BIRD

*This spinning helicopter-like contraption can be made quickly with just a few, easy to find items.*

## WHAT YOU WILL NEED:

Unsharpened pencil with eraser
Thumbtack
1-1/2 inch x 16 inch strip of thin cardboard

## HOW TO CONCOCT IT:

1. Place the middle of the cardboard strip centered on top of the pencil eraser.
2. Secure the cardboard strip onto the eraser of the pencil using a thumbtack.
3. Bend each end of the cardboard strip up to form a "V" shape.
4. Launch the Whirly Bird high into the sky by rolling the pencil between your hands and releasing it.

## CONCOCTION TIPS & IDEAS:

◆ Make your Whirly Bird more interesting by using a pencil with a unique design on it and by coloring the cardboard strip with felt tip markers or crayons.

# WHIRLY BIRD INSTRUCTIONS:

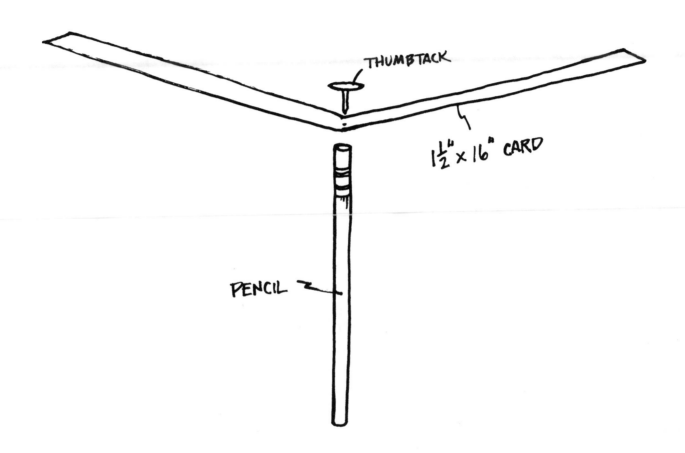

THUMBTACK

$1\frac{1}{2}$" × 16" CARD

PENCIL

# SEA MONSTER FARM

*Although they look like tiny sea monsters, these cute and amazing little creatures are actually brine shrimp.*

## WHAT YOU WILL NEED:

1/2 tsp. brine shrimp eggs (available at your local pet store)
5 tsp. kosher salt
Fish bowl
2 quarts tap water

## HOW TO CONCOCT IT:

1. Fill the fish bowl with 2 quarts of water. Let the water sit for 3 days. This process will allow the chlorine gas, found in most city water, to escape.
2. Pour the salt into the water and stir until the salt is completely dissolved.
3. Add 1/2 tsp. brine shrimp eggs to the water and then place the fish bowl in a warm spot.
4. The eggs will begin to hatch in about 2 days. They will continue to grow for several days until they become adults.

## CONCOCTION TIPS & IDEAS:

◆ Use a magnifying glass to observe your sea monsters as they hatch from their eggs and begin to grow.
◆ Turn off the lights and then place a small flashlight next to the fish bowl. As you move the flashlight back and forth the sea monsters will follow the light.

# SHRINKY DOOS

This wonderful shrinking art project is great for creating plastic key rings, earrings, and whatever else your imagination will allow.

## WHAT YOU WILL NEED:

1 white foam tray (the kind meat is packaged in from the grocery store)
Felt tip markers
Scissors
Tin foil

## HOW TO CONCOCT IT:

1. Wash the foam tray thoroughly with soap and water. Dry the tray with a paper towel.
2. Draw a picture on the tray with felt tip markers.
3. Use scissors to cut the picture out of the foam tray.
4. Have an adult put the foam picture on a piece of tin foil and place it in a pre-heated 200 degree oven for 5-10 minutes until the picture shrinks by 50%.
5. Have an adult remove the picture from the oven and allow it to cool for 20 minutes before handling.

## CONCOCTION TIPS & IDEAS:

◆ Try using black foam trays and draw designs with gold & silver paint pens.
◆ Use Shrinky Doos to create package ties, greeting cards, and book markers.

# Measurement Conversion Chart

| U.S. | Metric |
|------|--------|
| 1/4 teaspoon | 1 ml |
| 1/2 teaspoon | 2 ml |
| 1 teaspoon | 5 ml |
| 1 tablespoon | 15 ml |
| 1/4 cup | 50 ml |
| 1/3 cup | 75 ml |
| 1/2 cup | 125 ml |
| 2/3 cup | 150 ml |
| 3/4 cup | 175 ml |
| 1 cup | 250 ml |

# Food Coloring Blending Chart

| Colors | Food Coloring |
|---|---|
| Teal | 3 drops red + 2 drops green |
| Orange | 3 drops yellow + 1 drop red |
| Purple | 3 drops red + 2 drops blue |
| Light Green | 3 drops green + 1 drop yellow |
| Dark Red | 3 drops red + 1 drop blue |
| Gold | 4 drops yellow + 1 drop red |

# Index

# Contraptions

# Flying Contraptions

# Paint Concoctions